Where Insomnia and The Music Meet

Esmeralda Olivares

BookLeaf Publishing

India | USA | UK

Presentation by *BookLeaf Publishing*

Web: www.bookleafpub.com

E-mail: info@bookleafpub.com

ISBN: 9789363315761

First edition 2024

For the ones who feel too much in a world that cares too little. For the hopeless romantics who spill their hearts out through music.

If you relate to this, you are seen. You are loved. You are wanted. Always be who you are.

ACKNOWLEDGEMENT

Thank you to my best friend, who always
believed in me.
To the friends who enjoy my ramblings.

Thank you to my inner child, for always feeling
too much and always wanting to share. This is
for you.

WHERE INSOMNIA AND THE MUSIC MEET - COMPLETE SPOTIFY

PLAYLIST :

1. Sun and Moon: Glitter & Crimson - All Time Low
2. Curious Soul: Work of Art - Downer Inc.
3. Tired: Never Ending Nightmare - Citizen Soldier ft. Kellin Quinn
4. Break: deepfake - brakance
5. Bright Eyes Realize: Flourish - Osatia
6. Feeling of Home: Homesick (Acoustic) - Dayseeker
7. Life With You: Sabes - Reik
8. Untitled: Perfect Harmony - Julie and The Phantoms
9. My Prayer: Fall For Me - Sleep Token
10. Untitled II: Enchanted (Taylor's Version) - Taylor Swift
11. Do You Feel It Too?: Crush - David Archuleta
12. Changes: Todo Cambio - Camila
13. I'm All In: 10 I See - John Michael Howell
14. The First Kiss: Can We Kiss Forever? - Kina
15. Scared: I'm Yours - Alessia Cara
16. Trust Me: Feel Me Now - Derrick Ryan
17. All of Him: I Think I'm In Love - Taylor Acorn

Sun and Moon

He was the sun
Radiating his light
His warmth engulfed the entire world

She was the moon
Only comfortable in the dark

Different and beautiful on their own
But when they share the same sky
Something amazing is created

The sun and moon
What a cliche

But one can make it or break it
So my love, let's make it through
Only me and you

Curious Soul

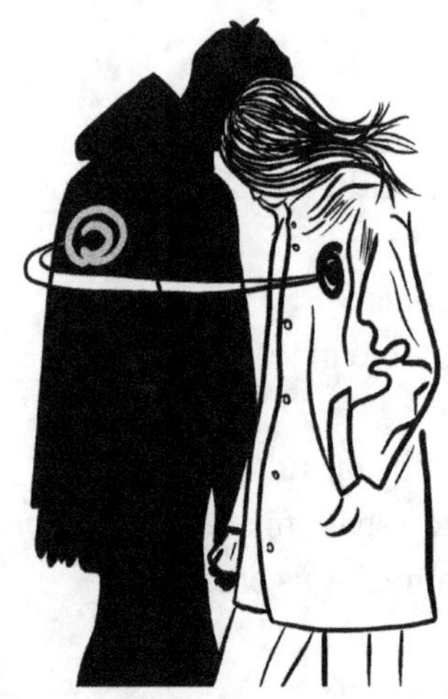

I am a curious soul
I like to experience and see new things
Wonders from around the world
Dangers excite me
Like lightning storms
And driving a bit too fast
Playing my music too loud
Just enough to risk hearing loss by age 30

My heart seemed to take its time
For love was never an option
Despite feeling some sort of attraction
These feelings usually died in the blink of an eye
And then I met you

When my eyes saw you
I thought, "Yeah, you're cute"
I swear it could've been momentarily
But seeing your smile
Your passion
Your hurt
Hearing your voice and confidence
I knew I was fucked

Excuse the language
There's no other way to describe it
The way my heart fell
I feel it in my gut
And I can see something more

Remember, I'm a curious soul
This could be dangerous
Risking heartache
But I'm willing to take it
Because you and I
I feel like we're music
Melody and harmony

Tired

I'm tired
I'm exhausted
"It's because you don't sleep"
And why do you think that is?
"You drink coffee all the time"
"Stop sleeping so late"
"You're always up until 3am"
If you only knew

If only they knew what goes through my mind
The tears I cry
The heaviness in my chest
My heart hollow
My body numb
Yearning for home
Hoping for change
Praying for rest

Break

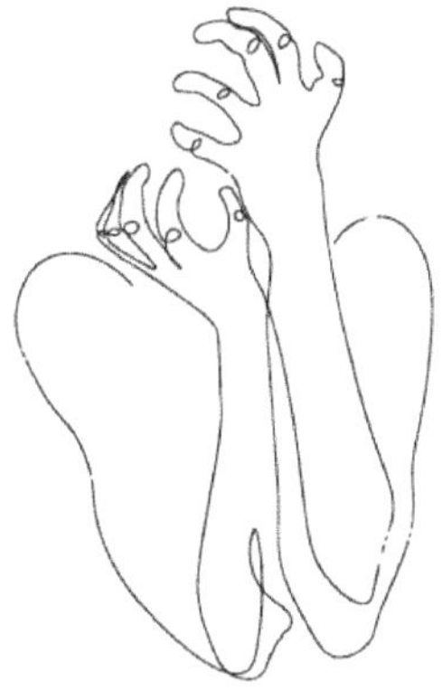

I'm tired of routine
The expectations
The fake smiles
Tired of playing pretend
Wipe the tears
No one can see you cry
You're the strong one
You've never needed anyone

Well maybe for once I want to break
Maybe I finally want someone
Someone to hold me when I fall
A shoulder I can cry on
A smile that melts my heart
A voice that soothes my nightmares
Two arms wrapped around me
Someone who makes me feel at home

Who am I kidding?
I write stuff like this
None of it exists
Simply fairy tales
Don't bother wishing
You'll only break your heart
Keep your head up
You have to keep fighting
But...

I'm tired

Bright Eyes Realize

Late night drives
Getting ourselves lost
To the beat of the music
Our hearts become one

Your hand in mine
I thought we were never-ending
Yet to the world we didn't exist
Two renegades on the run

I wanted it to last
The odds were against us
You had a different plan
While I was stuck on a feeling

I didn't want to let you go
Scared of being alone again
Yet I still wanted you to be happy
Even if I wasn't there

I'm driving down the road
Hands on the wheel
Dazed eyes fixed on bright lights

Feeling of Home

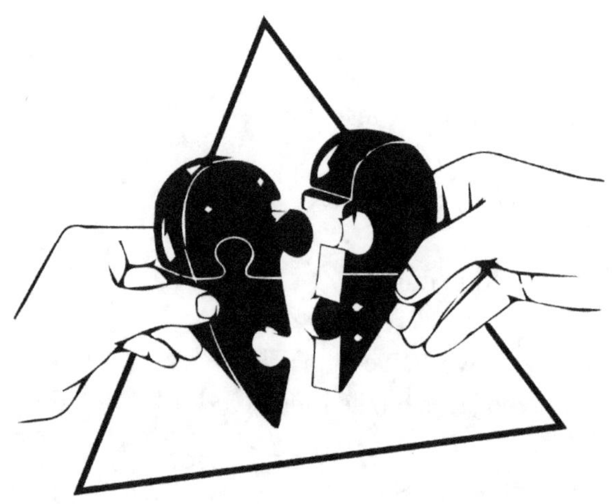

There's this boy
He's not perfect
But the way his eyes light up
Every time he talks about his passions and
interest
His crooked smile warms a heart I thought I'd
lost
His voice calms my fears and quiets the voices
that surround me
Allowing me to get through the night
Oh, how I can imagine his arms around me
Making me feel safe
Like I belong

So there's this boy
Though he's not perfect, I can assure you
He is to me
Not because he makes me whole
I learned a long time ago that people do not
serve that purpose
But to teach me to love
To be vulnerable with no fear
To trust without a doubt
He's not perfect
But he's home

Life with You

I want my life with you

I want lazy Sunday mornings with waffles and coffee
I want car rides with the music blasting, both of us singing in perfect harmony
I want rainy days, sitting on the porch, enjoying the rain
I want us dancing in the kitchen at 2 am because we couldn't sleep
I want walks along the beach, hand in hand, the moon shining on us like a spotlight
I want cozy days, reading/playing games while the day is gray

I want to make sure every moment with you creates a special memory
Because in all honesty, I never wanted anything more in my life than you.

Untitled

I want us to be the love story the poets envy to write about

And the love song the artists wish they could sing

My Prayer

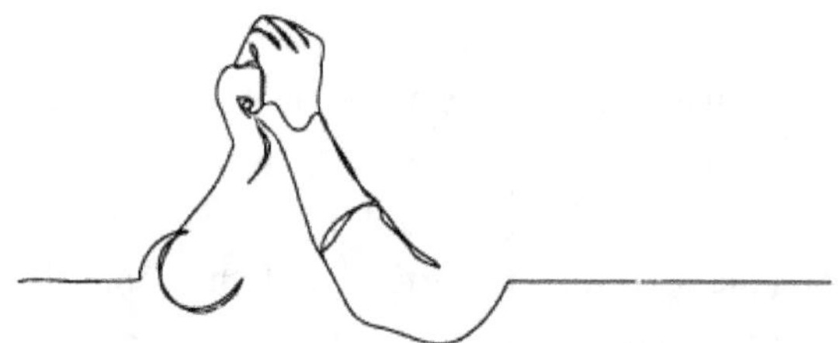

If only you knew you are who I prayed to God
for every night

If only you knew you are the one who has been
in my dreams

If only you knew you are the one who quiets my
mind when everything is loud

If only you knew how scared I am to be open yet
you make me feel safe

If only you knew how much I think about you

If only I knew how much of me you would
actually love...

Untitled II

Meeting you was a surprise

Being friends was easy

But falling for you was unexpected

And I'm forever enchanted

Do You Feel It Too?

I wonder if you see me in the same light I see
you.
If you feel what I feel with the same intensity

I love our friendship
Appreciate that I have you in my life

But I can't help but wonder if we can be more.
If everything that happened has been leading up
to more

And I want to be honest, I don't want to bottle
anything up.
But what if I read into this the wrong way?

I want to tell you, let my feelings out so that the
angels can hear.
God knows how I feel

But I'm terrified.
Do you feel the same?

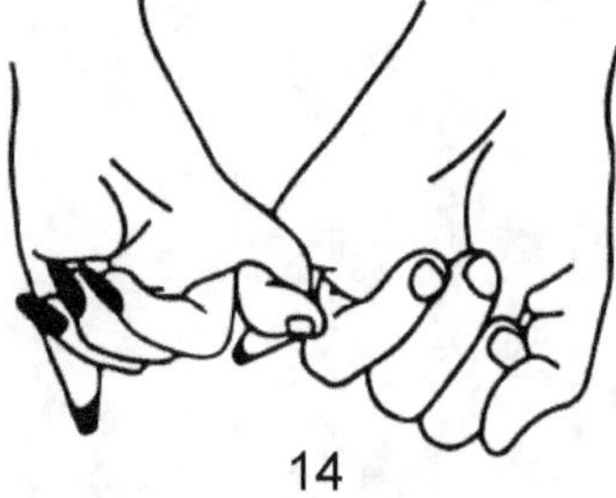

Changes

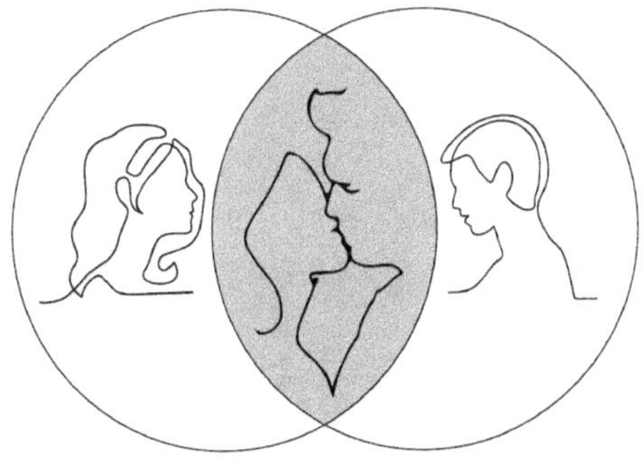

You changed me

In ways I never thought possible

I'm hoping again

I have dreams again, illusions for a better day

You lift me up with no hesitation

I didn't know I was looking for you, didn't expect this

But here you are, taking me as I am

You changed my way of thinking but I took the step to be better

I'm All In

I'm all in

Once I'm interested, I'm invested
I'm loyal once you become my friend
You won't lose me
I'll love you through your worst
Through the times you feel like you're drowning,
I'm here
I'm your biggest supporter
Reminding you how much you matter
I will always wait for you

It takes a lot to get me to open up
But it only takes you doing something stupid to
start losing me
Break my trust, stab me in the back
Throw the worst things at my face
And it'd be like I never knew you

I'm all in
But I'll also be all out if you push too far

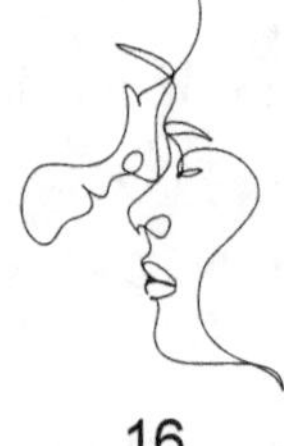

The First Kiss

I heard somewhere that it's not always about the
first kiss

It's about the first one that matters

And though my first wasn't perfect

Darling, I know the first with you will be
otherworldly

Scared

I'm scared

Scared of what I'm feeling
Scared of admitting to them
Scared of potentially ruining it
Ruining our friendship
Because what if it doesn't work?

But I'm also scared of ruining what could
happen
I'm scared of self-sabotaging
Scared of not giving it a chance
Because what if it does work?

What if it's better than I could imagine?

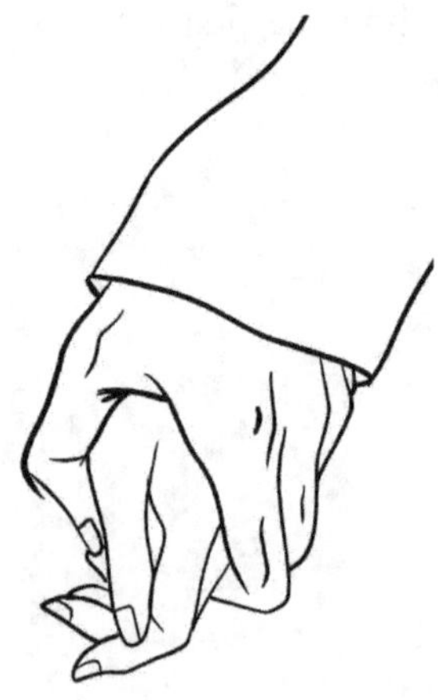

Trust Me

I promise I won't hurt you

I know you've heard it from others
I know you have your heart guarded
You're scared of being vulnerable
Of being let down
Life hasn't been too kind to you
And you've been incredibly strong
Your good heart and kindness hasn't wavered

I won't hurt you
I promise that you'll always have a shoulder to
cry on
Someone who will understand
Someone you can count on

Trust me
I won't break your heart

All of Him

What do I admire about him?

His smile
How his eyes light up
His laugh
How easy it is to have a conversation
His kind heart
How he sees the good in people
His caring nature
How he won't start a fight but will defend
anyone who needs it
His strength
I love how he stays true to himself
No matter what the world does to him

I admire him
Fully and completely, all of him

The Truth

To tell you the truth
I like you

You get me
You make me laugh
You make me smile
You make me happy
You know when I'm in my head
You know when I'm sad
You know me
My mannerisms, quirks, addictions

You make me feel safe
I'm comfortable with you
I can be myself
I can be vulnerable
Cry and tell you my worries
I can trust you

I really like you
You have no idea how much

Purely With You

They say sex is pure intimacy
The pinnacle of it all
But pure intimacy can be achieved in ways that
doesn't require having to get naked with
someone

It can be through the simple act of holding hands
Of the shy kisses that make us smile
Through the long hugs that can put our broken
pieces back together

Listening to our favorite songs and knowing the
reason why it is
Through the music that makes us cry, dance,
reminisce our past
Watching our comfort movies, the ones from our
childhood, the ones that got us through that hard
breakup

It can be achieved by just cuddling, soft touches
of skin and hair, nothing rushed, just enjoying
each other's presence
Cooking your loved one's favorite food when
they are sick
Baking together to make life a little sweeter
Dancing together, even if you're stepping on
each other's toes
Singing to each other in the car during long
drives or when one can't sleep at night
Making each other laugh until our sides hurt and
we're catching our breaths

Intimacy doesn't have to be sensual or even
physical
Just be present with your person

I'll Give You Everything

I'm willing to risk it all

I was so used to forgetting feelings
Cutting ties as soon as I saw it wasn't for me
Never willing to try more
Guess you could say I have a problem with
commitment
But when it comes to you

God, for you
I'll keep trying
I'll break down walls
Be more than friends
I'll keep waiting for a sign
I'll wait for the green light
I will be better

All for you

Shattered Glass and Splattered Paint

She is neither poised or elegant
For the war she's been fighting has left her a
wounded soldier

Her scars of shattered glass and her marks of
splattered paint reveal her story more than her
words could ever

Open Your Eyes

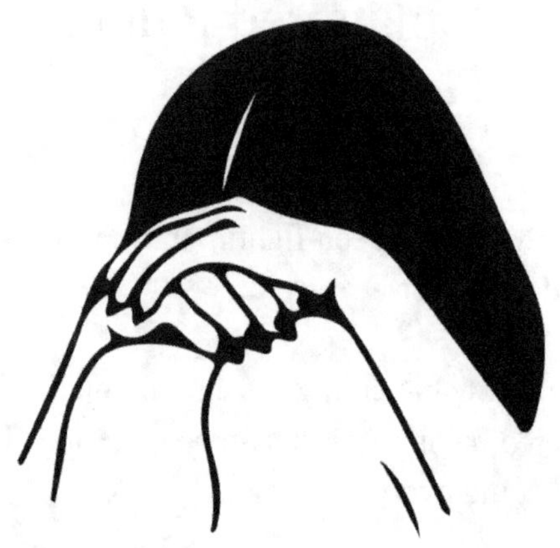

Open your eyes
Time is running out
Time marches on
And we want to live in the past

That happy little girl is long gone
All is left are broken dreams and empty hopes

Open your eyes
I beg, I plead, I implore
Don't be blinded to the reality
Because this isn't a dream

In fact, this is a nightmare
But there is no waking up

Open your eyes
Can't you see we're suffering
"Ignorance is bliss"
Then why do I feel dead?

Hey! Listen
I'm trying to talk
But my words fall silent to you

Open your eyes
Look at the sadness you've left
The abandonment in these tired eyes
Tired of silent cries

So many nights have passed
And you didn't even hear the sobs

Please
Open your eyes
Before it's too late
And I close mine

See me
I'm trying to get to you
Open them

Your Storm

I prayed for you
Like I prayed for rain

Others have taken shelter
But I'd rather dance in your storm

Honesty

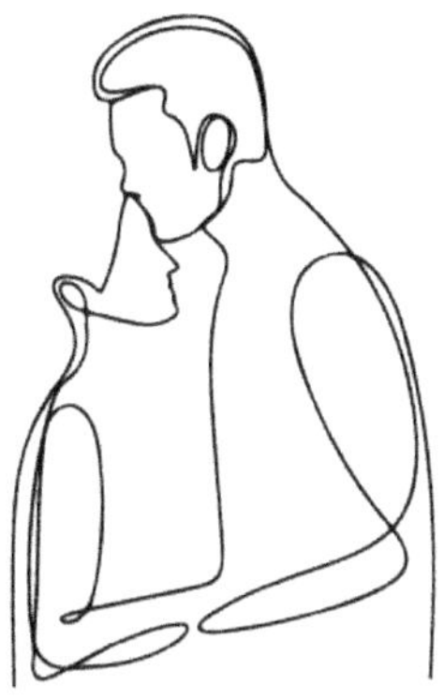

Be honest with me
That's all I ask

What are we doing?
Do you really care?
Are we friends?
Could we be more?

You don't have to call me 24/7
Hell, you don't have to text me every day
Just tell me you're alive

Let me know you're okay

Don't tell me you miss me
Then turn around and act like you can live
without me

Just be clear with me
And don't break my heart

I'm tired of hoping

I'm Trying

I'm not perfect
I have my bad days
I get emotional
I get defensive
I get tired
I don't know how to ask for help
I always thought vulnerability was a sign of
weakness

But I'm trying
All I ask is patience
Meet me halfway
Put in the effort when I can't
I won't always smile
I will cry when I'm overwhelmed
Life hasn't been fair and I'm fighting

I've always believed that a relationship is a team
Putting in the extra effort for one another
I'll be there for you, even if it'll break my heart
Please don't do the worst
Because I trust you enough to let you in

I'll show you my darker, weaker sides
Be there for me, don't let me fall

Missing You

I miss you

God, I missed you so much
If only you knew how happy you make me
Every conversation, every text, every look
I can't help but smile
I love hugging you because I feel safe
I never hug guys but with you…
I never want to let go

I wish I knew what you think
What your heart feels
I want to tell you but I'm terrified of ruining
what we have
I want you to know that my life became better
because you're in it

You might be scared that you'll hurt me
You might want to push me away
But you won't
I'll always be here for you

Heart in Ruins

I want to be honest
I want to tell you how I feel
I wish this was a movie where it happens
But the truth is…
This is real life

I'm not that great
There's better out there for you
There's someone who is better
I think you believe you'll ruin me
But I feel like I don't deserve you

I can't give you more
I'm so closed off
Can't even admit my feelings
Pretend that I don't need anyone
I might just push you away
And you don't deserve that

My own fear and doubt will ruin you
Just as it's ruined me

Gravity

You're not gonna ruin me
Life already did that
I was considered heartless for so long
I've been told I wouldn't understand certain
things
Because I don't feel like everyone else does

And I didn't care
I figured I was destined to be alone
And I was okay with that
Happy with it

But when I met you, something clicked
I thought it only happened in books
Yet there I was

Pulled into your gravity
Finding solace in you

I was never comfortable with anyone
But with you, I knew I could be
I'm willing to let my walls down
Let myself be helped and cared for

Show You Off

Let's take silly pictures together
Snapchat videos of happy memories
Ones that we post everywhere
Showing each other off

Let's take late night drives on the highway
Nothing but headlights as we get lost
Sunny days down the coast, hand in hand
Our voices singing along to the music

Let's have lazy days when we share comfortable
silence
I'm reading, head on your lap as you play video
games
Let's bake and cook in the kitchen
Arm around my waist as shy kisses are shared

Dancing every once in a while because you
know I'm a sucker for that

Let's show each other off
Coffee, movie, and bookstore dates
Prove to ourselves that our pasts didn't define us
That we are the better we hoped for

Safe With Me

Be vulnerable with me
Show me your scars
And I'll show you mine

Trust me with your heart
I'll protect it
As you do the same with mine

We'll tell our ghost stories
Clean out the skeletons in the closet together
No need to hide our darkest secrets

We'll have days when we hold each other tight
Sometimes the weight of the world gets a little
too heavy
Soft touches to remind ourselves that we have
each other
Kind words to block out the echoes of the
cruelty that surrounds us

Feeling Too Much

It's gonna be a pain
Dealing with me
My silence speaks volumes
I won't show my feelings unless I'm pushed

It's taken me years to realize
I do need someone
Someone I can depend on
Because I am exhausted

Don't tell me to shut up when I'm yelling

Believe me, it's not towards you
I'm holding too much in
And I will blow up

Don't tell me to stop crying
Let me feel it all
My feelings were invalidated for so long
I want to stop pretending

I need help
But I won't admit it
So please be patient
Because I don't know how long I can go

Soul Searching

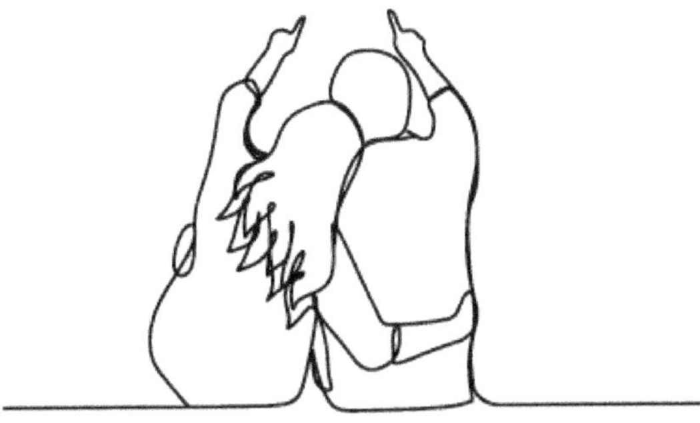

He felt a serenity enter his soul
Her soul, battered and beaten, was calm yet on
fire
He began to understand why she had such a
spit-fire attitude
The passion within her consumed her entire
being, ready to be set free
Hesitant to let go, afraid to fall
Wanting to avoid failure and heartbreak
He knew she would take the world by storm
If she decided to let it all go with no hesitation

She had been speechless, her mind ran in circles
There was something familiar with his soul
It ran wild but there was comfort
As if he was a forest and she felt safe being lost
in him
He was like the ocean, untamed and soothing

And she wouldn't mind drowning in him
He was like the rush and excitement of her
favorite song, blasting as she danced
around

Their souls were a cool summer breeze as the
sunset bled through the clouds
Warm and cool hues painting the sky
A work of art only God could create

After You

You have no idea how much it physically pains
me that you think so little of yourself
That past relationships have hurt you so much
you think you're a bad person
It hurts me to see you go quiet for days, fighting
your battles
It hurts that I wish you would talk to me
I want to help you

You say you don't deserve it but you do
You deserve every damn good thing that comes
your way
You have the kindest soul
The most caring heart I have ever known

And I wish you could see that
That you won't brush it off as if I was lying
I'm not

You don't want to worry me with anything
But having me in your life, worry is part of the
package
I care so much about you
I want to help you see your worth
I pray for your happiness
I pray for you to have someone who could
understand you
Who would be there for you through it all

I want you to know that I will always be by your
side no matter what

I will always be in your corner
Cheering you on
I want you to know that you will always have
someone to lean on
I will always care for you, even when you push
me away
Nothing will change that

Future

I want that real love
Us against the world
With God as our center

I want that real love
The one when people see us together
They know we were destined for each other

God made us go through life to find each other
Knowing we would need each other
Grow together
Be better together

Dance With Me

I wish I could send you all the songs that remind
me of you
The songs that I dedicate to you
The ones that speak my mind

And I know you'll smile and enjoy them
Even if you don't know or understand the words
fully
I can't help but even share the Spanish ones

You'll laugh and call me cute because of my
wide smile
Giggling and kicking my feet
Because the excitement I feel is towards you

You say you don't dance, but you would for me
Because I'm playing Bachata while cleaning
And all you want to do is see me smile
Completely comfortable in our goofiness